A Visual Dictionary of

Native Communities

Bobbie Kalman

🍄 Crabtree Publishing Company

www.crabtreebooks.com

Crabtree Visual Dictionaries
Created by Bobbie Kalman

For Aunt Joli and Uncle Laci,
sok köszönettel és szeretettel

Author and Editor-in-Chief
Bobbie Kalman

Editor
Robin Johnson

Research
Crystal Sikkens

Design
Bobbie Kalman
Katherine Kantor

Production coordinator
Katherine Kantor

Photographs and reproductions
© Dreamstime.com: page 19
© Bob Coronato/
  The Greenwich Workshop, Inc.:
  front cover
Artwork from PicturesNow.com:
  page 31 (left)
Alredo Rodriguez: Weaving Lesson:
  page 23
© Shutterstock.com: pages 30,
  31 (corn and maple leaves,
  pumpkin, and turkey)

Illustrations
Barbara Bedell: front cover (totem pole, drum, tipi, and rattle), back cover (girl, left basket, and warrior), pages 1 (top and middle baskets, stew, mother and child, stretching hide, seed beater, canoe, and horn), 3 (side moccasins, steatite carving, throwing stick, and basket), 4 (bottom left and right), 5 (girl gathering berries, basket, and stew), 6 (bottom), 7 (all except top left), 8 (all except top and middle right), 9 (all except Onondaga, Oneida, and Cayuga headdresses), 14 (all except signing buffalo), 15 (all except Pawnee, Blackfeet, and Sioux), 17 (girls playing), 18 (natives on raft and bottom home), 19 (necklace, moccasins, and water basket), 21 (all except basket, bundles of maize, and eagle), 24 (dip net), 25 (all except bark skirt, shell money, mortar and pestle, and sweat lodge), 26 (all except boxes), 27 (all except whale oil and blanket), 28 (family), 29 (man and woman), 30, 31 (making pottery)
Katherine Kantor: front cover (bowls, basket, inukshuk, and moccasins), back cover (prayer stick), pages 3 (pots, cactus, and tortillas), 5 (man, woman, headdress, moccasins, and pots), 6 (top), 9 (Onondaga, Oneida, and Cayuga headdresses), 11 (all except fur cap, regalia, and longhouse), 12 (bottom left), 13 (top left), 18 (agave), 21 (bundles of maize), 23 (cactus), 24 (acorns and balsa), 25 (bark skirt, sweat lodge and mortar and pestle), 28 (ivory saw and sod house), 29 (inukshuk)
Trevor Morgan: page 29 (seal)
Bonna Rouse: back cover (pottery), pages 3 (side pottery), 4 (ice fishing and map), 5 (village), 8 (top), 11 (longhouse), 17 (tipi), 18 (cactus), 20, 21 (eagle), 22, 23 (beans), 24 (bottom right), 28 (top igluvigak and blanket toss), 31 (top)
Margaret Amy Salter: front cover (shield, buffalo symbol, hanging food, snowshoes, and dreamcatcher), back cover (moccasins, quills, right basket, and bird art), pages 1 (pottery, rattle, dreamcatcher, box, bottom basket, and club), 3 (buffalo symbol, top pottery, top moccasins, native person, basket with corn, shell money, and regalia), 6 (middle), 7 (top left), 8 (middle right), 10, 11 (fur cap and regalia), 12 (all except bottom left), 13 (all except top left), 14 (signing buffalo), 15 (Pawnee, Blackfeet, and Sioux), 16, 17 (all except tipi and girls playing), 18 (club and wickiup), 19 (calendar stick, fiddle, bow, and basket), 21 (basket), 23 (prairie dog and horse), 24 (salmon), 25 (shell money), 26 (boxes), 27 (whale oil and blanket), 28 (bottom igluvigak), 29 (all except inukshuk, man, woman, and seal)
Tiffany Wybouw: page 31 (cranberries)

Library and Archives Canada Cataloguing in Publication

Kalman, Bobbie, 1947-
   A visual dictionary of Native communities / Bobbie Kalman.

(Crabtree visual dictionaries)
Includes index.
ISBN 978-0-7787-3505-2 (bound).--ISBN 978-0-7787-3525-0 (pbk.)

   1. Indigenous peoples--North America--History--Dictionaries,
Juvenile. 2. Indigenous peoples--North America--History--Pictorial
works--Juvenile literature. 3. Picture dictionaries--Juvenile literature.
I. Title. II. Series.

E76.2.K34 2007   j970.004'97003   C2007-906598-8

Library of Congress Cataloging-in-Publication Data

Kalman, Bobbie.
   A visual dictionary of Native communities / Bobbie Kalman.
      p. cm. -- (Crabtree visual dictionaries)
   Includes index.
   ISBN-13: 978-0-7787-3505-2 (rlb)
   ISBN-10: 0-7787-3505-2 (rlb)
   ISBN-13: 978-0-7787-3525-0 (pb)
   ISBN-10: 0-7787-3525-7 (pb)
   1. Indians of North America--History--Dictionaries, Juvenile. 2. Indians of North
America--History--Pictorial works--Juvenile literature. I. Title. II. Series.

E76.2.K35 2008
973.04'97--dc22

2007044419

Crabtree Publishing Company
www.crabtreebooks.com   1-800-387-7650

Published in Canada
Crabtree Publishing
616 Welland Ave.
St. Catharines, Ontario
L2M 5V6

Published in the United States
Crabtree Publishing
PMB16A
350 Fifth Ave., Suite 3308
New York, NY 10118

Published in the United Kingdom
Crabtree Publishing
White Cross Mills
High Town, Lancaster
LA1 4XS

Published in Australia
Crabtree Publishing
386 Mt. Alexander Rd.
Ascot Vale (Melbourne)
VIC 3032

Contents

Native nations coast to coast

Native peoples were the first peoples to live in North America. There were many native **nations**, or groups. The people of each nation spoke different languages, wore different styles of clothing, and practiced their own customs and traditions. The native peoples had different ways of life, too. They found food in different ways and built their own styles of houses, depending on where they lived. Some native nations lived near oceans. Others lived near forests or in deserts. Some nations lived far north, in the cold Arctic. In this book, you will meet some of the native peoples who lived throughout North America.

ice fishing

Some native peoples lived in the freezing Arctic. They fished through holes in the ice and built snow houses (see pages 28-29).

ARCTIC OCEAN

ARCTIC

ARCTIC CIRCLE

PACIFIC OCEAN

NORTHWEST COAST

CALIFORNIA COAST

WESTERN GREAT LAKES

EASTERN GREAT LAKES

GREAT PLAINS

NORTHEAST

SOUTHEAST

SOUTHWEST

ATLANTIC OCEAN

*Some native nations hunted **bison**, or buffalo. They followed the animals from place to place, taking their belongings with them. They ate the meat of the buffalo and used their **hides**, or skins, to make clothing, blankets, and homes (see pages 14-17).*

Some native peoples fished in oceans and found clams on beaches (see pages 26-27).

clams

4

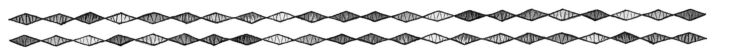

Life of the Powhatan

The Powhatan nation was made up of many groups of people who lived in the Tidewater region of what is now Virginia. Some lived on the coast of the Atlantic Ocean. Some lived on rivers and other waterways that flowed into the ocean. At first, the people hunted animals and gathered foods. They moved from place to place looking for animals and plants to eat. Later, they began growing their own **crops**.

beaded headband →

shell jewelry

← breechcloth

painted designs

Men and women wore clothes made from soft deer hide. Men wore **breechcloths**, and women wore dresses. They both wore jewelry made of shells. For special occasions, they decorated their bodies with painted designs.

Girls helped gather fruits and other foods.

*This **headdress** was worn by a Powhatan leader. It was made of feathers and deer hair.*

headdress

*People wore shoes called **moccasins**.*

canoes

*Powhatan houses were called **yi-hakans**.*

*The Powhatans lived in villages that were built beside water. They built large homes that held many people. People traveled in boats called **canoes**.*

Powhatan women wove strong baskets.

They cooked hearty stews made from meat or fish.

Food was stored in pots made of clay, seashells, and stones.

5

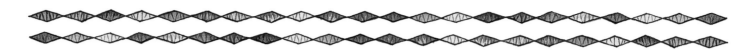

Eastern Great Lakes

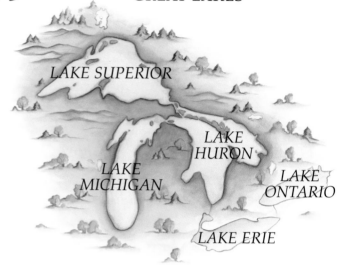

Many native nations lived in the eastern Great Lakes region. They built **permanent** villages around Lake Ontario, Lake Erie, and east of Lake Huron. They also traveled throughout their **territories**, hunting, fishing, and gathering food. Most of the nations that lived in this region belonged to two **confederacies**. A confederacy is a group of nations that join together to reach common goals and to stay peaceful. The Haudenosaunee Confederacy and the Wendat Confederacy were made up of several nations that spoke similar languages. Other groups in this region, such as the Eries, the Neutrals, and the Tionontati, were **allies**, or partners, of the Wendat.

bear

*Each person belonged to a **clan**. A clan was a group of people who believed they shared an **ancestor**. The ancestor was represented by the spirit of an animal, such as a bear.*

There were many lakes and forests in the eastern Great Lakes region. The lakes and forests provided people with the water, food, and materials they needed. People used materials from nature to build homes and boats and to make clothing and tools.

corn squash beans

Women were in charge of planting crops. The main crops were corn, squash, and beans. These plants were called the "three sisters" because they helped one another grow.

Meat was hung on racks over a fire. The smoke from the fire preserved the meat and kept it from going bad.

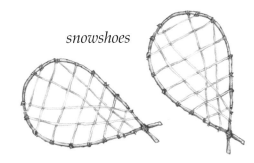

meat

smoke

pestle

mortar

Dried corn was put into a **mortar** and pounded with a **pestle**. The ground corn, called **cornmeal**, was used to make corn bread.

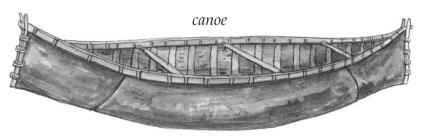

canoe

In warm weather, people traveled on rivers and lakes in canoes. The canoes were made of birch wood and bark.

snowshoes

In winter, people strapped **snowshoes** onto their feet. The snowshoes kept them from sinking into the snow. They pulled goods through the snow on **toboggans**.

toboggan

longhouse

In the eastern Great Lakes region, people lived in villages made up of homes called **longhouses**. These wooden homes were built next to rivers and streams. Several families lived in one longhouse. The families were usually from the same clan.

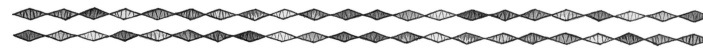

The Haudenosaunee

The Haudenosaunee were made up of five nations: the Mohawk, the Oneida, the Cayuga, the Onondaga, and the Seneca. The five nations lived, hunted, fished, and grew crops in territories that were side by side. They **settled**, or lived, on the southern shores of Lake Ontario and in the Finger Lakes area of New York State. There, the nations built longhouse villages along the water. The name "Haudenosaunee" means "people of the longhouse."

Many families lived together in one longhouse. They also stored their food and belongings in the longhouse.

The Haudenosaunee had a lot of fun! They liked to dance and sing songs. They used **water drums** *and rattles made from turtle shells to make music.*

water drum

rattle

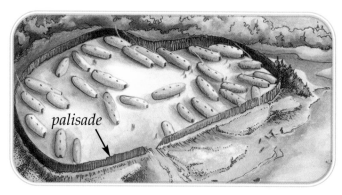

palisade

Longhouse villages were surrounded by **palisades**. *Palisades were walls made of sharp poles. The palisades prevented other nations from attacking the Haudenosaunee.*

The Haudenosaunee gathered food from the land. In spring, they collected **sap** *from maple trees and boiled it to make maple syrup. They used syrup instead of sugar.*

The **elders** *of the longhouse were grandparents or older aunts and uncles in the village. People respected the elders and enjoyed listening to their stories.*

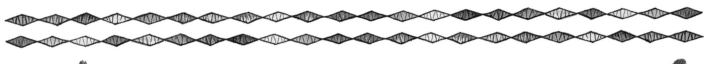

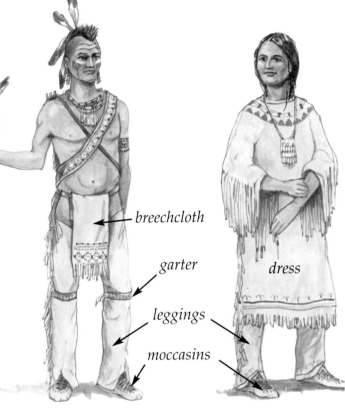

breechcloth

garter

dress

leggings

moccasins

robe

Mohawk

This man's hairstyle, known as a "Mohawk," was created by **tweezing** and shaving areas of hair so only a single row was left at the top.

In summer, men wore breechcloths and women wore leather dresses or skirts. Neither wore shirts. In winter, both men and women wore hide shirts or jackets, leggings wrapped with garters, and robes made from animal fur. They wore soft hide moccasins on their feet.

hapes

Hapes were symbols that the Haudenosaunee painted on their faces or bodies. These symbols had important meanings.

gustoweh

A headdress called a **gustoweh** was sometimes worn by a man to show his nation. Each nation had a different design and was identified by the number and position of the feathers.

This headdress belonged to the Onondaga nation.

A man from the Oneida nation wore this headdress.

The Cayugas were recognized by this headdress.

9

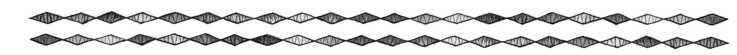

Western Great Lakes

Many native nations lived in the western Great Lakes region. They settled around Lake Superior and Lake Michigan and west of Lake Huron. Nations in the western Great Lakes region had different homes, clothing, languages, and customs and traditions. They shared similar **lifestyles**, or ways of life, however. They fished, hunted, and gathered foods from the land. Different foods were available as the seasons changed, so people moved from place to place. They traded goods they had for items they needed or wanted.

clay pot

dried corn

dried fish

*Members of the western Great Lakes nations lived in large groups made up of several **extended families**. Extended families include grandparents, parents, children, and other family members. This family is gathered together inside a **wigwam**.*

canoe

People in this region often traveled by canoe. Nations, such as the Menominee and the Potawatomi, built large, heavy canoes for traveling on rough waters.

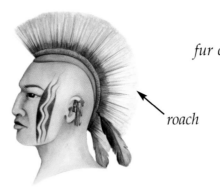

The men of the Fox nation sometimes wore **roaches**, or special headpieces, during battles. The roaches were made from porcupine quills or deer fur.

roach

fur cap

To keep warm in the winter, some people wore pieces of deer skin or fur caps on their heads.

wigwam

Most nations used wigwams as their winter homes. Wigwams were **portable** and easy to set up. The frames were made from trees and were covered with bark, hides, furs, or **reeds**. Reeds are tall woody grasses. The coverings were the only parts of the wigwams that people took with them when they traveled.

regalia

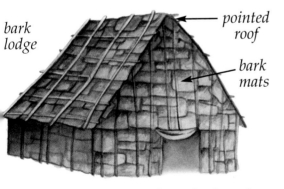

bark lodge

pointed roof

bark mats

The Ho-Chunk, Menominee, Sauk, and Potawatomi all lived in similar houses called **bark lodges**. The wooden frames were covered with bark or reed mats. The Potawatomi and Menominee **lodges** had pointed roofs.

The Kickapoo carved symbols of their beliefs onto wooden prayer sticks.

Regalia were special items people made or had given to them for acts of bravery or good deeds. Regalia could be weapons, tools, bags, or belts.

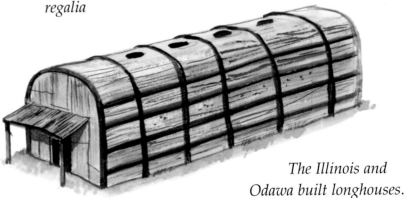

longhouse

The Illinois and Odawa built longhouses. Longhouses in this region were rectangular wooden buildings with rounded roofs. They were covered in bark.

The Anishinabe

The Anishinabe lived in territories in the western Great Lakes region. Like other nations in this region, the Anishinabe nation was made up of many groups of extended families. Families moved with the seasons in search of food and natural materials. They used the natural materials to make clothing, shelters, tools, and other supplies.

wigwam

The Anishinabe built wigwams for both summer and winter use. Several families lived in a large summer wigwam, whereas only one family lived in a small winter wigwam.

toboggan

In winter, men hunted and caught fish through holes in the ice. They carried their supplies on toboggans. Women stayed with the children inside the wigwams. They made clothing and other items during this time.

birch bark

container

In spring, people cut and peeled the bark from birch trees. They used the birch bark to make containers, canoes, and shelters.

wild rice

*In the fall, people gathered the grains of grasses known as **wild rice**. Wild rice was one of the Anishinabe's most important foods.*

In summer, many families set up large camps together. The men hunted, fished, and built canoes. The women dried meat and fish and gathered food from the forests. Most women also planted vegetable gardens.

The Anishinabe played games with their families and friends. They especially enjoyed playing a game we now call **lacrosse**. They played lacrosse for fun, as part of religious ceremonies, and to settle arguments.

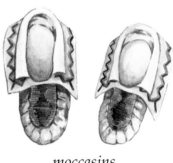

Anishinabe men wore breechcloths in summer and long leggings and hide shirts in winter. Anishinabe women wore long hide dresses all year long. In cooler weather, they added sleeves to their dresses and wore hide leggings.

The Anishinabe believed dreams contained important messages. To help receive good dreams, some people made **dreamcatchers**. The hole in the center of the dreamcatcher let the good dreams pass through to the dreamer. The web around the hole caught the bad dreams. When the sun rose, it burned the bad dreams away.

dreamcatcher

Moccasins were made from moose or deer hide. They were often decorated with dyed porcupine quills.

moccasins

Girls learned many things from their mothers and female family members. This mother is teaching her daughter how to bite designs into birch bark. Making birchbark designs was a favorite hobby.

Fathers taught their sons valuable lessons. They showed them how to hunt, fish, and make items such as weapons, tools, and canoes.

13

Nations of the Plains

Dozens of native nations lived on the Great Plains. The Great Plains is a huge, flat, grassy area of land. There were few trees and other plants there, and water was hard to find. Nations that lived on the Plains relied on buffalo for their food, clothing, and homes. Some **nomadic** peoples followed the buffalo as they roamed across the Plains. Others were **sedentary**, or lived mainly in one place. Sedentary nations lived near water on the edge of the Plains. They hunted near their villages or took short hunting trips in search of buffalo.

tipi

*Many families lived in lightweight tents called **tipis**. The tipis could be taken apart easily and carried from place to place.*

earth lodges

sod

*Some Plains peoples lived in permanent villages. They built houses called **earth lodges**. Earth lodges were made of wood and were covered with **sod**. Sod is soil that has grass growing on it.*

sign for buffalo

*Many Plains nations spoke different languages. To communicate with one another, they used **sign language**. Sign language is a way of talking by moving your hands in special ways. This sign means "buffalo."*

Before horses were brought to North America from Europe, native peoples traveled on the Plains by foot. They used dogs to help carry their tipis and other supplies. After the arrival of horses, some sedentary nations became nomadic. Native peoples could travel more easily across the Plains on horseback.

Mandan

Arikara

Pawnee

Assiniboine

The Mandan, Arikara, and Hidatsa nations lived in permanent earth lodge villages. They grew corn, beans, and squash. They often traded these crops for buffalo hides.

The Pawnee nation lived in earth lodges. They grew crops and went on hunting trips in search of buffalo and deer.

The Assiniboine were nomadic peoples that traded furs with the Europeans.

Blackfeet

Sioux

Comanche

Crow

bangs →

The Blackfeet nation was a large, powerful nation of warriors. They had nomadic camps with colorful tipis. They wore decorated outfits.

The people known as the Sioux were part of a large confederacy. They grew crops and also hunted. Later, part of the nation became nomadic and only hunted buffalo.

The Comanche traveled on horseback. Their warriors wore feathered headdresses and carried decorated weapons and shields.

The Crow were farmers at first. Later, they became nomadic. They wore decorated outfits and styled their bangs to stand upright.

Plains camp life

Nomadic nations lived in camps on the Great Plains. The camps were made up of tipis that could be set up and taken down quickly and easily. Groups of families lived together in the camps. Although each family had its own tipi, families shared food and **resources** with one another. The most important resource was the buffalo they hunted. People in a Plains camp used every part of the animal. The meat of the buffalo was their main source of food. They used buffalo hides and bones to make clothing, shelter, tools, and weapons.

jerky

Buffalo hides were stretched tightly and scraped clean. After the hides dried in the sun, they were used to make shelter, clothing, bedding, drums, and shields.

stretched hide

*After a buffalo hunt, people cooked and ate fresh meat. The rest of the meat was dried and made into **jerky**. People ate jerky when no fresh meat was available.*

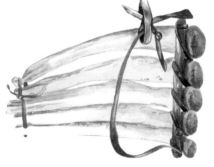

Toboggans were made by tying buffalo ribs together.

Spoons were made from buffalo horns.

*Shields were made of buffalo **rawhide**. Rawhide is a stiff, hard leather made from buffalo skin.*

Men wore buffalo headdresses during ceremonies and while fighting in battles.

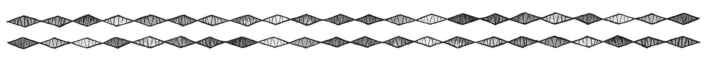

hot stone

Stones were heated in a fire and placed in a rawhide case filled with water. The hot stones cooked soups and stews.

bullboat

Bullboats were used for traveling on rivers. They were made by stretching buffalo hides over willow branch frames.

smoke hole

tipi

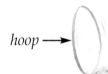

hoop

spear

Plains children played with toys that helped them learn important skills. The boys above are playing a game that helps them practice hitting a moving target. This game taught Plains children how to become good hunters and warriors.

Tipis were made of long poles covered with buffalo hides. Everyone and everything had a special place inside a tipi.

inside a tipi

Furry buffalo hides, called **robes**, were used as beds and placed around the fire.

The fire was in the center of the tipi, directly below the smoke hole.

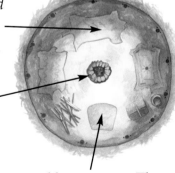

These girls are learning how to put up a tipi by practicing on a small toy tipi. They are also learning to be mothers by taking care of their dolls.

Each tipi was owned by a woman. The seat opposite the door was reserved for her husband or for important guests.

Nations of the Southwest

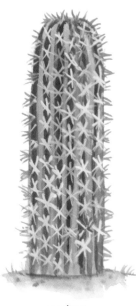

cactus

The Southwest region is made up of present-day Arizona, New Mexico, and parts of Utah and California. Nations that lived in this hot, dry region understood the land and how it could supply them with the things they needed. People that lived near rivers built permanent villages. They grew squash, beans, and **maize**, or corn, on the land around their homes. Nations that did not live near water were nomadic. They lived in **temporary** shelters and hunted elk, deer, coyotes, and other animals throughout their territories. They gathered cactuses, agaves, and other wild plants as they traveled.

agave

People of the Southwest used the fruits and seeds of plants to make food and medicine.

club

People often used wooden clubs to hunt small animals. They used bows and arrows for larger animals.

pole

raft

The Mohave were among the few Southwest nations that fished for food. Mohave men used rafts and poles to travel to fishing spots. There, they used nets and baskets to catch fish.

wickiup

*Some Southwest nations lived in temporary shelters called **wickiups**. Wickiups had wooden frames. The frames were covered with grass.*

In the villages of the Akimel O'odham and Tohono O'odham nations, people lived in large homes. The homes had willow frames that were covered with brush and mud.

18

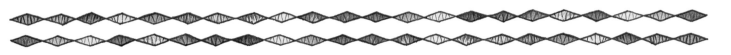

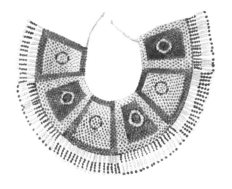

The people of the Tohono O'odham nation carved cuts and symbols of important events onto **calendar sticks**.

The Quechan nation made valuable necklaces out of beads. The necklaces were often used in trading.

The Apache people wore high moccasins that often curled up over their toes.

bow

The Apache used the stalks of yucca plants to make instruments known as "Apache fiddles." The fiddles were colorfully painted and were played with bows.

fiddle

water basket

The Walapai were skilled basket makers. They made many styles of baskets, including those that held water. Water baskets were coated with a layer of **pitch** to keep the water from leaking out. Pitch was made from pine sap.

fruit

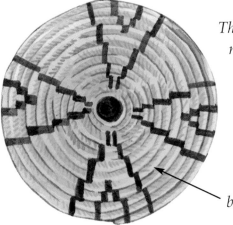

The people of the Yavapai nation mainly hunted and gathered food. Very few were farmers. They made beautiful baskets and pottery.

basket

Some Southwest nations gathered the fruit of the saguaro cactus. The fruit could be eaten fresh or used to make jam and syrup. It was also used to flavor drinks.

Pueblo life

Many nations of the Southwest lived in **pueblos**. Pueblos were large, permanent homes that had several **levels**, or floors. They were made by stacking stones or **adobe** bricks. Adobe is a mixture of clay, straw, and water that hardens when it dries. Pueblos were sturdy buildings that lasted many years and housed many families. Entire villages could live in large pueblos, such as the one shown below.

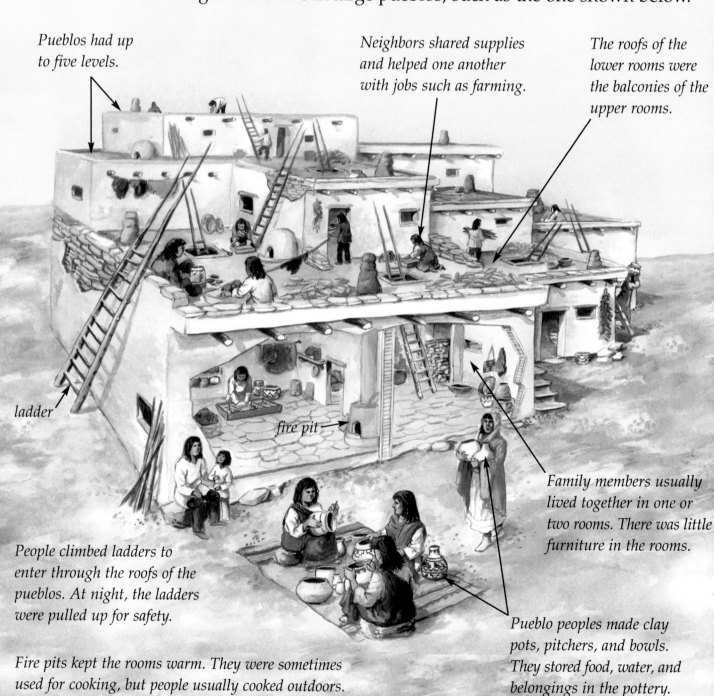

Pueblos had up to five levels.

Neighbors shared supplies and helped one another with jobs such as farming.

The roofs of the lower rooms were the balconies of the upper rooms.

ladder

fire pit

Family members usually lived together in one or two rooms. There was little furniture in the rooms.

People climbed ladders to enter through the roofs of the pueblos. At night, the ladders were pulled up for safety.

Pueblo peoples made clay pots, pitchers, and bowls. They stored food, water, and belongings in the pottery.

Fire pits kept the rooms warm. They were sometimes used for cooking, but people usually cooked outdoors.

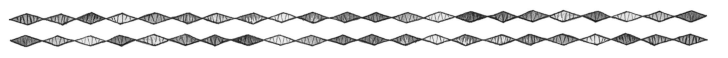

bundles of maize

Pueblo peoples planted crops near their homes. They relied on maize and other foods for their survival.

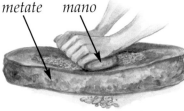

metate   mano

Beans, nuts, and dried corn were often ground together using a **mano** and **metate**.

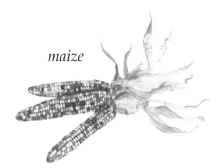

maize

Baskets were woven out of leaves, grass, roots, or bark. People wove yucca fibers to make waterproof baskets.

In warm weather, men wore **aprons**. In cold weather, they wore shirts, leggings, robes, or skirts called **kilts**.

eagle

Eagles and hawks were caught and raised by hunters. People used the feathers of these birds in ceremonies.

apron   manta

Women wore **mantas**, or cotton dresses, throughout the year. When the weather turned cold, women also wore robes or blankets.

sandals

For most of the year, people wore sandals made from yucca plants. In cool weather, they wore socks with the sandals. People wore moccasins during cold winter weather.

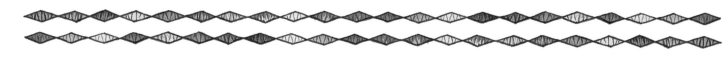

hogan

The Navajo

The Navajo were a Southwest nation. Like other nations in this region, they knew how to survive in a hot, dry **climate**. The Navajo were **seminomadic**. They lived in different winter and summer camps. They hunted and gathered wild foods, but they also grew vegetables and fruits on farms. Most Navajo farmers were **flood farmers**. They farmed only during the summer months, when their fields were flooded by rainfall or by water from rivers. Many Navajo families also raised sheep and goats. The animals provided them with meat, milk, and **fleece**, or wool. The Navajo spun the wool into yarn and made beautiful clothing, blankets, and rugs.

*Most Navajo families lived in **hogans**. Early hogans were low cone-shaped buildings that were covered with clay. The hogans stayed warm in winter and cool in summer.*

A typical Navajo family was made up of a mother, a father, and their unmarried children. The family usually lived near other family members.

decorated blanket

*Early Navajo people wore clothing made from deer hides. In later times, the Navajo used woven cloth or knitted wool for making clothes. The men wore pants, and the women wore dresses. They also wore colorful decorated blankets and **sashes**.*

sash

*Mothers carried their babies with them wherever they went. They used **cradleboards** to keep their babies safe. The babies were wrapped in blankets and tied to the boards. Mothers took the babies out every few hours so they could stretch and move.*

cradleboard

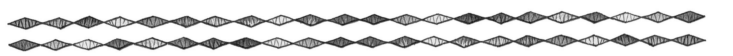

The Navajo wove blankets on **looms**, or wooden frames. They used the blankets for sleeping, for keeping warm, for making dresses, and for carrying objects.

Navajo farmers grew maize, squash, beans, and fruits such as peaches.

beans

The Navajo gathered wild berries, seeds, herbs, and fruits from cactus plants.

prickly pear cactus

prairie dog

The Navajo hunted deer, rabbits, mountain goats, prairie dogs, and other **game**. Game are wild animals that people hunt.

Horses were important to the Navajo people. The Navajo traveled on horseback to hunt and gather foods that were far from their camps. They also used horses to carry goods and to visit family members who lived far away.

horse

The California coast

dip net

Several native nations lived on the coast of what is now California. They found plenty of food and natural resources in the Pacific Ocean and in **inland** forests, or forests away from the coast. Native peoples in this region lived and worked in **bands**. Bands are groups of family members who speak similar languages and have similar customs and traditions. The bands of the California coast lived in **village groups**. A village group was made up of one or more large main villages surrounded by a group of small villages. Each village group had at least one **chief**, or leader. He or she offered advice, settled disagreements, and made important decisions for the village.

Chinook salmon

*People of the California coast fished throughout their territories. They used large **dip nets** to catch salmon, trout, and other fish in lakes, rivers, and streams.*

balsa

*Some native people used rafts called **balsas** to travel in calm or shallow waters. Balsas were made by tying long stalks of **tule** tightly together. Tule is a plant that grows near water.*

acorns

*Many bands in this region gathered **acorns** in the fall. Acorns are nuts that grow on oak trees. Some bands traveled long distances to reach acorn **groves**, or places where many oak trees grow. The acorns were used to make breads, cakes, soups, and other foods.*

24

bark skirt

Trees were valuable to the California coast nations. People used the wood and bark from the trees to make canoes, shelters, weapons, and clothing, such as this woven bark skirt.

throwing stick

This wooden throwing stick was a weapon used to hunt rabbits and other small animals.

seed beater

Many California bands were skilled basket makers. This basket was known as a **seed beater**. It was used to knock seeds off bushes.

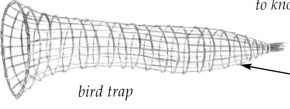

bird trap

This woven trap was used to catch birds.

ramada

Ramadas provided shade from the sun. People sat underneath them to keep cool while they worked.

pelican carving

People used **steatite**, a soft soapstone, to carve bowls, utensils, pipes, and animal models, such as this pelican.

shell money

shell necklace

Shells were plentiful on the California coast. They were used as money in trading. Jewelry, such as earrings and necklaces, was also made from shells.

sweatlodge

Sweatlodges were steam baths used by men for ceremonies. They were also gathering places for talking and praying. The sweatlodges were built into the sides of streams or creeks or were partly underground.

pestle

mortar

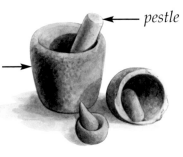

Mortars and pestles were made from stone. They were used to pound, grind, and mix foods.

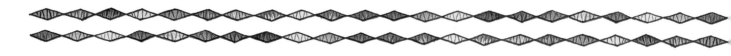

The Northwest coast

The Northwest coast is a narrow strip of land that lies between the Pacific Ocean and the Coast Mountains. It stretches from the northern part of what is now California to the southern part of what is now Alaska. Much of this area is now part of Canada. The climate in this region is mild and wet. Native nations found plenty of food and natural resources in the ocean, rivers, and **rain forests** of this region. Salmon and cedar trees were the most important resources. Some salmon was caught, cooked, and eaten fresh, but most was preserved to last for months. Cedar was used to make houses, canoes, tools, weapons, and **totem poles**.

Totem poles are tall wooden statues. The animals carved on the statues represent native stories and events.

houses

totem poles

canoes

cedar boxes

People of the Northwest coast lived in villages made up of large wooden houses. The houses were built in rows facing the ocean and were shared by many people. Native people fished, hunted, and collected resources in the territories around their villages.

bark strips

The bark of cedar trees is made up of two layers. The inner layer is soft and stringy. Native people shredded the inner bark into thin strips. The strips were woven to make baskets, blankets, and other items. The hard outer layer of the bark was used to make boxes and bowls.

bark boxes

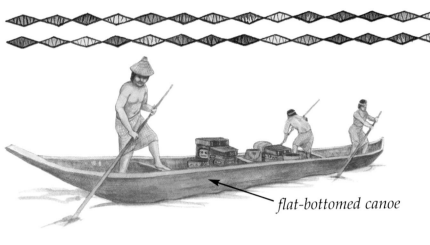

flat-bottomed canoe

People of the Northwest coast traveled mainly by canoe. Each village owned hundreds of canoes that were made for different waterways and different tasks. **Freight canoes** were made to carry heavy loads of food and supplies. Two canoes were sometimes joined to carry big loads.

This flat-bottomed canoe was made for traveling on streams. Long poles were used to push and steer the canoe through shallow water.

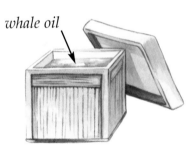

freight canoe

In winter, there were strong winds and heavy rains. **Plankhouses** were built using sturdy cedar wood, which did not rot in wet weather. Totem poles, called **house frontal poles**, stood at the entrances of the homes.

house frontal pole

The Makah people were whale hunters. They used whale oil to preserve and prepare food. Whale oil was a valuable trade item.

whale oil

plankhouse

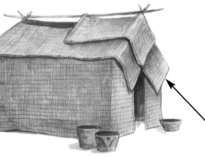

In the southern part of the region, huts were made using woven mats of cedar bark or reeds. These huts were used in hunting or fishing camps.

bark or reed hut

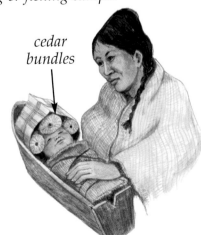

cedar bundles

wool blanket

The Northwest coast nations ranked their people as nobles, commoners, or slaves. The nobles and commoners had high, flat heads. To create this shape, mothers tied bundles of cedar to the foreheads of their babies.

The Chilkat were part of the Tlingit nation. They made beautiful blankets from the wool of mountain goats. The blankets were used in ceremonies and for trade.

The Far North

The Far North is a huge area of land and water north of the Arctic Circle. It includes the Yukon, Nunavut, and the Northwest Territories, which are in Canada. Parts of Alaska are also in the Arctic. The climate in this region is very cold and windy. Snow and ice cover the ground for most of the year, and very few plants grow. Despite these harsh conditions, two native nations have lived in the Far North for hundreds of years. The Inuit and the Inupiat nations knew how to survive using the natural resources in this cold, snowy land.

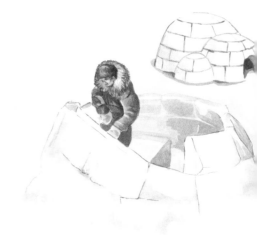

*Some Inuit lived in snow houses called **igluvigak**. The Inuit cut and stacked blocks of hard-packed snow to build these homes.*

*The Inuit used **ivory** snow saws to cut the ice for their igluvigak. Ivory came from walrus tusks.*

ivory snow saw

Inuit and Inupiat families lived, traveled, hunted, and worked together.

blanket toss

sod house

*The Inupiat and some Inuit lived in **sod houses** during the winter. Sod houses were made by putting whalebone frames over hollows in the ground. Layers of stones and soil were placed over the frames.*

*During winter, people had fun playing games such as **blanket toss**. In this game, a walrus hide or sealskin was held by its edges and lifted into the air. People took turns jumping on it. It was like a trampoline!*

Mothers carried their babies in large hoods, called **amauti**.

amauti

hooded parkas

mittens

pants

boots

The Inuit made human-shaped statues called **inukshuks**. Inukshuks were built to show where people had traveled or hunted.

inukshuk

harp seal

The clothing of men and women was similar. Both wore several layers of clothing made from various animal furs and hides. They wore hooded **parkas**, fur mittens, and waterproof pants. Their boots, called **mukluks** or **kamiks**, were made from sealskin or caribou hides.

The Inuit and Inupiat hunted seals, whales, fish, caribou, polar bears, and other animals. They ate the meat of the animals and used their hides for clothing. They found uses for almost every part of an animal.

ulu

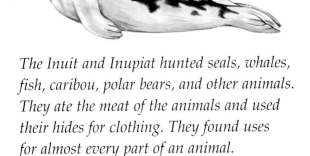

Women in the Far North used knives called **ulus** to chop meat, to break up ice, and to scrape hides clean.

spear

Hunters used spears and other weapons. **Floats** kept the spears from sinking in ocean waters.

float

People of the Far North carved beautiful works of art from ivory, bone, and antlers.

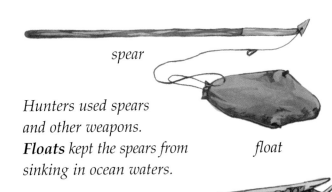

umiak

oil lamp

Oil lamps were carved from large stones. Seal oil was used to light the lamps.

People traveled through ocean waters in large boats called **umiaks**. They traveled along the coasts in small covered boats called **kayaks**.

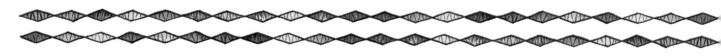

Native wisdom

The native nations of North America lived in different regions and had different lifestyles, but they shared important beliefs. They understood and respected the land, water, plants, and animals in their territories. They never hunted, fished, or gathered more than they needed. They lived in harmony with nature and offered thanks for its gifts to them. The wisdom of the nations has been passed down from one **generation** to the next. It has been told in stories, songs, dances, and art for thousands of years.

Native people did not hunt animals when the animals were having their babies. People knew that if they did so, there would be fewer animals in the future.

*Native people knew the plants that grew in their territories and used some of them as medicines. When explorers sailed to North America, many had **scurvy**. Scurvy is an illness caused by not having enough vitamin C in the body. The native people gave the sailors tea made from evergreen branches. The tea cured their scurvy.*

Family was important to all native nations. Each family member had an important role in the home and in the community. Older people lived with their children and grandchildren. They were respected for their wisdom.

drypainting

Native nations held different ceremonies or rituals to give thanks. This Navajo ceremony, called the Blessing Way, used **drypaintings** to bring good health and happiness to those who celebrated it. The patterns for the paintings were passed down through the generations.

Children did not go to school. They learned important life skills by watching their parents and working with them. Parents taught children how to make the things they needed in life. This girl is learning how to make pottery from her mother.

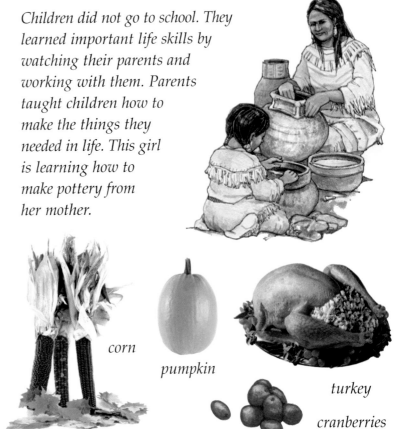

corn

pumpkin

turkey

cranberries

Many of the foods we eat today were first eaten by native peoples. Corn, maple syrup, cranberries, beans, pumpkins, wild rice, salmon, and turkey are just a few of these foods.

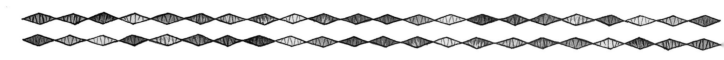

Glossary

Note: Many boldfaced words are defined where they appear in the book or are shown by pictures that are labeled.

ally A group that is friendly with another

ancestor An ancient relative or animal spirit from which one is believed to be descended

clan A group of families that share an animal spirit, such as a bear, as their ancestor

climate The usual long-term weather in an area

confederacy An association of two or more groups that have common goals

crop A plant grown for human use

elder An older or wiser respected member of a family, group, or nation

generation A set of family members that were born at about the same time, such as children

nation A large group who shares a common language, origins, history, and traditions

native Describing people who were born or have lived in an area for a long time

lodge A native shelter

nomadic Describing people who live in camps and move often to follow the animals they hunt

permanent Describing something that is meant to last a long time

plankhouse A house made of wooden boards

portable Describing something that can be carried

rain forest A thick forest that receives a lot of rain

resource Something natural or human-made which is useful or valuable to people

sap A sweet liquid found in trees, especially maple trees, from which syrup is made

sedentary Describing people who settle permanently in an area

seminomadic Describing people who live in permanent homes but also travel to find food

settle To stay in a place and make a home there

temporary Describing something that lasts only for a short time

territory An area of land and water on which a group of people live, hunt, and gather food

tweeze To pluck or pull hair out of the skin

Index